Real E Math Workbook

A Reference Guide for All Real Estate Math

- ✓ *Calculations*
- ✓ *Rules of Real Estate*
- ✓ *Detailed Examples*
- ✓ *Easy to Understand Explanations*

Listen on the Go with Real Estate Audio Prep 🎧
Scan the QR code below to Begin Listening ↓

Highly Rated by Real Estate Agents!

Table of Contents

Your Certification is Our Reputation

At Easy Route Test Prep, our Focus is on your Success. We understand you're not just preparing for an exam; you are laying the groundwork for a successful career in real estate. Our goal is to equip you with *practical tips, essential tools, and insightful guidance* to excel on your exam and in your future endeavors as a real estate agent.

Our Story . . .

Easy Route is a test preparation company that was created to help aspiring professionals become certified. The idea for Easy Route started with a simple question that I asked myself after taking my first licensure exam to become a real estate professional...

What would have been helpful for me while I was preparing?

I started putting my notes together, researching, and summarizing the essential information needed to become a real estate agent. Real estate materials can be overwhelming, and it's often unclear what to focus on while studying. This guide was created to take the guesswork out of preparation. Our philosophy is simple. . .

Study Intently → Practice Deliberately → Become Real Estate Agent

This forms the basis of every product we offer, whether it's our comprehensive *Study Guides, Audio Prep* materials, or the insightful *blog* articles I personally write. Each of these resources is crafted with the original goal in mind: *To provide the guidance and support that I wished I had during my own preparation.*

Thank you for investing your study time with us. I wish you all the best in your future endeavors,

Daniel Hile

~ Easy Route Test Prep

Basic Math Concepts

The basic concepts used in math are **addition, subtraction, multiplication, and division**. These concepts are applied through **calculations, equations, and formulas**. The calculations used in real estate and that will be asked on the exam are based on these basic concepts.

➢ A **calculation** is a mathematical determination of the size or number of something.

➢ An **equation** compares things that are equal to each other *(It will have an equal "=" sign)*

➢ A **formula** is a fact or rule that uses mathematical symbols. For example, The formula for Newton's 2nd law of motion states that force = mass x acceleration *(F = m x a)*

☑ **Tip**: When learning a new calculation practice reworking the equation to solve for each of its components. This is a great way to **enhance your practical applied knowledge** and double check that your answers are correct. Remember to round off calculations *(where applicable)*.

The T-Bar Method

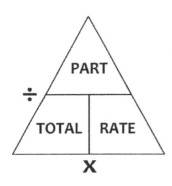

The "**T**" within the triangle represents the relationship between **PART, TOTAL, and RATE.** If the part is unknown then multiply, if the part is known then divide. The *horizontal* line is used for *division*. The *vertical* line is used for *multiplication*.

Calculating Commission

The following formulas can be applied using the T-Bar Method.

✓ **PART = TOTAL × RATE**

✓ **TOTAL = PART ÷ RATE**

✓ **RATE = PART ÷ TOTAL**

🔍 Example

You've closed on your first transaction as a real estate agent... Congrats! The sale price of the property is $500,000 and your portion of the commission is 2.5% of the sales price. In this scenario the sales price is the *total*, the commission rate is the *rate,* and the commission amount is the *part*.

How much did you earn from the sale?

☐ *Sales price ($500,000) × Commission rate (0.025) = Commission ($12,500)*

You earn $15,000 in commission on your next real estate transaction at the same 2.5% commission rate.

What was the sales price of the property?

☐ *Commission ($15,000) ÷ Commission rate (0.025) = Sales price ($600,000)*

Your next property sale nets you $24,000 in commission and the property sold for $800,000.

What was your commission rate?

☐ *Commission ($24,000) ÷ Sale price ($800,000) = Commission rate (0.03 / 3%)*

Conversions – Percentages and Decimals

Most real estate calculations use a percentage of something to determine a specified amount. You can convert a percentage into a decimal by dividing it by 100 *(50% ÷ 100 = 0.50)* or just move the decimal point two spaces to the left *(50.0% = 0.50 / 2.5% = 0.025 / 0.25% = 0.0025)*. You can convert a decimal into a percentage by multiplying by 100 *(0.50 x 100 = 50%)* or move the decimal point right two places *(0.50 = 50.0% / 0.025 = 2.5% / 0.0025 = 0.25%)*

Note: The percentages in the examples that follow reference standard ranges. These amounts can change depending on the circumstances. The *T-Bar Method* can be applied to calculate the unknown component of each.

- ☐ **Down Payments** are usually 20% of sales price

   $300,000 (Sales price) × 0.20 = $60,000 (Down payment)

- ☐ **Loan-to-Value Ratio** is typically 80% of appraised home value

   $300,000 (Sales price) × 0.80 = $240,000 (Loan amount)

- ☐ **Real Estate Commissions** range from 5% to 6% of sales price. *Commissions are usually split between the buyer and seller agents at 2.5% to 3% each*

   $300,000 (Sales price) × 0.05 = $15,000 (Total commission)

- ☐ **Discount Points** cost 1% of loan amount *(each)* and lowers the APR by 0.25%

  $240,000 (Loan amount) × 0.01 = $2,400 (Discount point cost)

- ☐ **Debt-to-Income Ratio** 28% front-end, mortgage payment / 36% back-end, all debts

  $10,000 (gross monthly income) × 0.28 = $2,800 (front-end, max mortgage payment)

  $10,000 (gross monthly income) × 0.36 = $3,600 (back-end, max for all debts)

- ☐ **Capitalization Rate (Cap Rate)** 5% to 10% is considered good

  $30,000 (Net operating income) ÷ $300,000 (Estimated property value) = 10% (Cap Rate)

Fractions

A fraction is a part of something. For example, in the fraction ¼ the bottom number *(denominator)* tells us the item has been divided into 4 parts, the top number *(numerator)* tells us we are working with 1 of those 4 parts. Fractions are not used as much in real estate but it's important to know how to convert them as well. To convert a fraction to a decimal, divide the top number *(numerator)* by the bottom number *(denominator)*.

- ✓ ¼ (1 ÷ 4) = 0.25 (25%)

- ✓ ½ (1 ÷ 2) = 0.50 (50%)

- ✓ ¾ (3 ÷ 4) = 0.75 (75%)

Formulas for Calculating Mortgage Interest

The timeframe for which a question is being asked is a good place to start when calculating interest. Mortgage payments are paid **monthly,** the interest is based on an **annual**-percentage rate (APR), and the loan term is based on a certain number of **years.** The values used to determine the interest amount are based on these time periods in relation to the principal *(loan balance)* and the rate of interest. The interest amount for each mortgage payment is based on the **monthly interest rate x the remaining loan balance (principal).**

🔎 Example

The starting mortgage loan amount is $600,000 for a property with an annual-percentage rate (APR) of 3.125% for a 30-year fixed loan. The monthly payment can be calculated using the amortization chart.

*($600,000 ÷ $1,000) gives you 600 x 4.28375 = **$2,570.25** (monthly mortgage payment)*

The **Total** interest can be calculated as follows:
- ✓ 30 years x 12 months = 360 total monthly payments
- ✓ $2570.25 x 360 = $925,290 total amount paid
- ✓ $925,290 - $600,000 = **$325,290 total interest paid**

The **Monthly** interest can be calculated as follows:
- ✓ 3.125% APR (0.03125) ÷ 12 Months = 0.260417% (0.00260417 monthly rate)
- ✓ $600,000 x 0.00260417 = $1,562.50 (1st months interest)
- ✓ $2,570.25 - $1,562.50 = $1,007.75 (1st months principal)

What would the principal + interest be for the 2nd mortgage payment?
- ✓ $600,000 - $1,007.75 = $598,992.25 (remaining principal balance)
- ✓ $598,992.25 x 0.00260417 = $1,559.88 (2nd months interest)
- ✓ $2,570.25 - $1,559.88 = $1,010.37 (2nd months principal)

Simple Interest Formula

Simple interest is a quick and easy method of calculating the interest charge on a loan. It is calculated using the principal only and ***does not include compounding interest.*** Simple interest is determined using the following formula

Simple Interest = P x R x T

P = Principal Amount

R = Rate of Interest per year

T = Time Period involved in months or years

🔍 Example

Using simple interest calculate the total interest paid on $10,000 borrowed at 5% annual interest for 5 years.

$10,000 x 0.05 x 5 = $2,500 Total interest paid

Property, Transfer, and Recording Tax

Calculating annual property taxes requires knowing the *appraised value, tax assessment ratio (varies by state), and tax rate.* Tax rates are expressed as a rate per dollar amount of value, such as $5 per $100 ($5 ÷ $100 = 0.05 tax rate) Tax rates can also be expressed as mills *(millage).* A mill equals 1/1000 of the assessed value of the property subject to property taxes. 50 mills is the same as $50 ÷ $1,000 = 0.05 tax rate.

> *Value × Assessment ratio = Assessed value*
>
> *Assessed value × Tax rate = Annual property tax*

🔎 Example

A property worth $640,000 is assessed at 40%. The tax rate is $20 per $1,000, or 20 mills.

> ➤ **$640,000 (property value) × 40% (assessment ratio) = $256,000 (assessed value)**
>
> $256,000 (assessed value) × 0.02 (tax rate) = $5,120 (annual property tax)

Transfer Tax is applied when real property is sold. Transfer tax rates vary by location, but the rate is usually a *percentage of the total sale price* or a *dollar amount per $1,000 of the sale price.* Make sure you know the transfer tax rate and calculation procedures in the areas where you practice real estate.

🔎 Percentage Example

A property sells for $450,000 with a transfer tax rate of 0.05%. First convert 0.05% to a decimal (0.05 ÷ 100 = 0.0005). Then multiply sales price by rate: **$450,000 × 0.0005 = $225**

🔎 Dollar Amount Example

A property sells for $525,000 with a transfer tax rate of $1.50 per $1,000 of the sales price.

> ➤ **($525,000 ÷ 1,000) gives you 525 × $1.50 (tax rate) = $787.5 (transfer tax)**

Recording Tax (Deed or Mortgage) is a tax on the recordation of the mortgage/deed of trust and is based on the sales price for a deed or the loan amount for a mortgage. Both taxes are usually quoted as an amount per $100, $500, or $1,000.

🔍 Deed Example

A property sold for $735,000 with a deed recording tax rate of $3.00 per $1,000.
How much is owed for the Deed of Recording Tax?

> ➢ **(735,000 ÷ 1,000) gives you 735 x $3.00 (tax rate) = $2,205 (recording tax fee)**

🔍 Mortgage Example

Using the example above calculate what the recording tax would be if the buyers financed $580,000 with a mortgage recording tax rate of $1.75 per $500.

> ➢ **(580,000 ÷ 500) gives you 1160 x $1.75 (tax rate) = $2,030 (recording tax fee)**

Proration – Allocating Expenses

Prorated items are shared expenses that are divided between the parties at closing. Prorated items will either be ***prepaid (have already been paid)*** or ***accrued (haven't yet been paid)***. If a question on your exam requires the calculation of prorated amounts, the question will specify whether the calculation should be made on the basis of a ***(statutory/banker's year = 360 days)*** or an ***(actual/calendar year = 365 days; 366 in a leap year)*** and whether the day of closing belongs to the buyer or seller. If using a statutory or calendar year isn't specified, calculate based on actual days of the corresponding calendar year. Calculate prorations with the seller responsible for closing day unless told otherwise. The following information is needed to calculate prorated items:

- ✓ *The per diem rate (per day rate)*

- ✓ *How many days each party is responsible for*

- ✓ *If the item is accrued or prepaid*

- ✓ *What time period is covered (usually annual)*

🔍 Property Tax Example

Property taxes are typically paid in *arrears (after)* meaning that the taxes paid on the due date are for the previous tax year. Your listing is under contract with a closing date of 7/8/24. The annual property tax bill of $3,484.32 is due in arrears on 12/31/24. Calculate the prorated amounts for the buyer and seller based on an actual calendar year with the closing date belonging to the seller.

➢ **$3,484.32 (total tax) ÷ 366 days (2024 is a leap year) = $9.52 (per diem rate)**

366 (days) - 177 (Jan 1st to July 8th 2024) = 189 (July 9th to December 31st 2024)

189 (days) x 9.52 (per day) = $1,799.28 (buyer prorated amount)

177 (days) x 9.52 (per day) = $1,685.04 (seller prorated amount)

🔍 Rent Example

A new tenant *(lessee)* is starting a lease agreement with the landlord *(lessor)*. The closing date is on April 4th 2024. The monthly rent is $2,400 due on the 1st of each month. Calculate the prorated amount the tenant owes for the month of April if the landlord *(lessor)* is responsible for the closing day.

➢ **Daily rent = $2,400 (monthly rent) ÷ 30 (days in month) = $80 (daily rent / per diem)**

30 (days in month) – 4 (days for landlord) = 26 (days for tenant)

26 (days) x $80 (per day) = $2,080 (prorated rent amount for April)

Buyer Funds

At closing, buyers are expected to have the funds available to meet the agreed upon purchase price in the contract. Buyers commonly use both **personal funds (cash)** for closing cost and down payments along with **lender funds (mortgage)** for the remaining balance. The **earnest money (good faith) deposit** from the buyer also goes towards the total amount due, usually as part of a down payment.

The required **'cash to close'** consists of the buyers down payment and closing costs, minus their earnest money and other credits. The estimated closing expenses are included in the initial **Loan Estimate (LE)** and the actual closing expenses are included in the **Closing Disclosure (CD).**

Common Buyer Closing Expenses

- ✓ *Lender fees*
- ✓ *Closing costs*
- ✓ *Recording fees*
- ✓ *Initial Escrow payment for the upcoming year's Property taxes and Insurance*

Depending on the closing date buyers may also owe interest at closing because the first monthly payment is generally made on the first day of the second month after closing. The interest is based on a per diem rate. The buyer will pay interest from the day of closing through the last day of the same month.

Example

The closing date on a property is June 21st with the buyers first mortgage payment due on August 1st. Remember mortgage payments are paid in arrears which means the payment made on August 1st is for the previous month of July. The buyer's loan is $540,000 with a 5% annual percentage rate (APR) and the closing day belongs to the buyer. Using a *statutory/banker's year* calculate the buyers interest owed at closing.

($540,000 × 0.05) = $27,000 (annual interest)

$27,000 ÷ 360 = $75 (per day interest)

$75 (per diem rate) × 10 (days) = $750 (interest paid at closing for the month of June)

Seller Proceeds

Calculating seller proceeds from a real estate transaction involves deducting commissions and other seller expenses from the sales price. If the seller still has a mortgage on the property, the closing officer ensures that the seller's loan and all interest is paid unless the buyer is assuming the loan. The loan interest is paid per diem *(per day)* for the month of closing.

⌕ Example

The sales price of a property is $450,000 with a 5% real estate commission rate. 100% − 5% = 95% or 0.95 (percent to seller).

$450,000 (sales price) × 0.95 (percent to seller) = $427,500 (net seller proceeds)

The closing date is November 20th and the seller agrees to pay $5,000 towards the buyer's closing cost. The seller also has a loan balance of $120,000 with a 3.84% annual percentage rate. The last mortgage payment was made on November 1st *(paid in arrears)*. *What is the total net proceeds for the seller after paying all debts and expenses?*

$427,500 (seller proceeds) - $120,000 (loan balance) - $5,000 (closing cost) = $302,500

3.84% (0.0384) APR ÷ 12 (months) = 0.32% or 0.0032 (monthly interest rate)

$0.0032 (monthly interest rate) x $120,000 (loan balance) = $384 (mortgage interest)

$384 ÷ 30 (days) = $12.8 (per day interest)

$12.8 x 20 (days) = $256 (mortgage interest owed)

$302,500 − $256 = **$302,244 (total net seller proceeds)**

Calculating Equity

Equity is the deference between the ***current market value*** of a property and the ***debt owed*** on the property *(loan balance)*. Equity increases by paying down the principal balance and / or by increased property market value. Equity decreases by depreciation *(decrease in market value)* and / or taking out additional home equity loans. On a mortgaged property equity and loan-to-value (LTV) have an inverse relationship.

As ***equity increases*** ↑ ***loan-to-value decreases*** ↓ and vice versa.

 Example

A couple is selling their primary home they purchased 10 years ago for $500,000. They currently have a loan balance of $400,000. The property has appreciated in value, and they are under contract to sell for $750,000. *How much equity have they accumulated?*

Current Property Value ($750,000) – Loan Balance ($400,000)
= Equity ($350,000)

Remember

✓ ***Appreciation*** in value ***increases equity*** ↑
✓ ***Depreciation*** in value ***reduces equity*** ↓

Determining Rental Property Depreciation

Depreciation is the process used to deduct the costs of buying and improving a rental property. Rather than taking one large deduction in the year a property is purchased or improved, depreciation distributes the deduction across the useful life of the property. Only the cost of the buildings on the land can be depreciated. Land can't be depreciated because it doesn't wear down. ***The Internal Revenue Service (IRS)*** has specific rules regarding depreciation:

- ✓ *The person claiming depreciation must own the property.*
- ✓ *The property must be used for an income-producing activity.*
- ✓ *The property is expected to last for more than one year.*
- ✓ *The property has a determinable useful life, meaning it's something that wears out, decays, gets used up, becomes obsolete, or loses its value from natural causes.*

U.S. residential rental property is ***depreciated at a rate of 3.636% each year for 27.5 years.***

Note: *This is based on current IRS rules which can change and there are exceptions to this rule.* The IRS provides instructions on how to depreciate property via its ***Publication 946.***

The first step in calculating depreciation is to **determine the cost basis** for the property. This includes the purchase price and certain closing costs that can be included such as *legal fees, recording fees, surveys, transfer taxes, and title insurance.*

The next step is to **separate the cost of land and buildings.** This can be based on the fair market value of each at the time of purchase, or the amount on the property tax assessment.

The final step is to **determine the annual depreciation** amount which is written off as an expense on annual tax returns. This decreases the total amount of taxes paid each year by the owner.

🔍 Example

A rental property was purchased for $700,000 with an additional $10,000 in allowed closing expenses. The cost of the land is assessed at $140,000 based on the property tax assessment. *What is the annual depreciation allowed for this property?*

➤ **$710,000 (total cost basis) - $140,000 (land value) = $570,000 (building value)**

$570,000 (building value) ÷ 27.5 years (useful life) = $20,727.27 (annual depreciation)

The total gross income of the rental property is $48,000 annually. The total expenses for the property are $12,000 not including depreciation. *What is the total annual taxable income?*

➤ **$48,000 (gross income) - $12,000 (expenses) - $20,727.27 (depreciation) = $15,272.73**

If in the 22% tax bracket, depreciation would save $4,560 *(rounded)* in taxes annually. ($20,727.27 x 0.22 = $4,560)

Land Measurement

Land measurements are stated in terms of *square feet, square miles, perimeter, frontage foot, linear miles, acres, and hectares.*

- ✓ **Front foot *(frontage)*** is the length of the property along a street, highway, or waterway.

- ✓ **Perimeter** is the length and width of all sides added together.

Conversions

- ➢ **1 Township** = 36 Square Miles

- ➢ **1 Square Mile** = 640 Acres (1 Section of a Township)

- ➢ **1 Acre** = 43,560 Square Feet ***Memorize for exam**

- ➢ **1 Hectare** = 107,639 Square Feet or approximately 2.47 acres

- ➢ **1 Linear Mile** = 5,280 Feet ***Memorize for exam**

Formulas

- • **Acres** = Square feet ÷ 43,560

- • **Square Feet** = Acres × 43,560

- • **Linear Mile** = Linear feet ÷ 5,280

- • **Linear Feet** = Linear Miles × 5,280

🔍 Land Size Example

A property is being subdivided into a land parcel that is a half-mile square. How many acres is this subdivision? Each side of the parcel is 2,640 linear feet (5,280 feet in a mile x 0.50).

2,640 × 2,640 = 6,969,600 square feet

6,969,600 ÷ 43,560 (square feet in an acre) = 160 acres

🔍 Land Value Example

A parcel of land is three-quarters of a mile by 3,190 feet. The price is $2,500 per acre. How much is the land worth?

5,280 feet × 0.75 (3/4 of a mile) = 3,960 feet

3,960 feet x 3,190 feet = 12,632,400 square feet

12,632,400 ÷ 43,560 (square feet in an acre) = 290 acres

$2,500 (price per acre) × 290 (acres) = $725,000 (property value)

🔍 Frontage Example

A parcel of land is 10,000 total sq ft and is 80 feet deep. What is the frontage?

10,000 (total area) ÷ 80 (feet of depth) = 125 (feet of frontage)

Metes-and-Bounds

Legal descriptions are characterized by a point of beginning, which is where the description both begins and ends.

- ✓ **Metes** are the direction and distance of a line forming the property's boundary.

- ✓ **Bounds** are physical features that *define the boundaries of the property*. The road "Conservation Drive" is a boundary in the example below.

- ✓ **Monuments** are permanent physical markers used in a metes-and-bounds description that can be man-made or natural. It may be a tree, creek, rock, or a stake placed in the ground. Monuments are used within a metes-and-bounds description to mark points at which there is a change in direction as one follows the boundary of the parcel. It also uses *monuments* to mark boundaries.

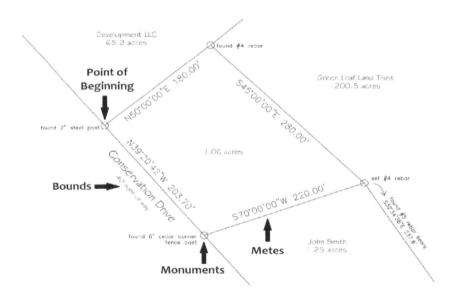

Metes-and-Bounds Written Description

"BEGINNING at a found 2" steel post, the west corner of this tract, the south corner of a 65.2 acre tract, and on the east right-of-way line of Conservation Drive; THENCE N50°00'00"E 180.00' with the south line of the 65.2 acre tract to a found #4 rebar, the north corner of this tract, and the west corner of a 1200.5 acre tract described in Volume 75 on Page 342, on the southeast line of the 65.2 acre tract; THENCE S45°00'00"E 280.00' with the west line of the 1200.5 acre tract to a set #4 rebar, the east corner of this tract, and the north corner of a 1.25 acre tract described in Vol. 5 on Page 273 of the Official Public Records, on the west line of the 1200.5 acre tract, and from which a found #5 rebar, the southeast corner of the 1.25 acre tract, bears S32°34'36"E 237.6'; THENCE S70°00'00"W 220.00' with the north line of the 1.25 acre tract to a found 6" cedar corner fence post, the south corner of this tract, and the west corner of the 1.25 acre tract, on the east right-of-way line of Conservation Drive; THENCE N39°20'42"W 203.70' with the east right-of-way line of Conservation Drive to the POINT OF BEGINNING, containing 1.06 acres of land."

The Rectangular Government Survey System (RGSS)

Also known as the Public Land Survey System (PLSS), is regulated by the **U.S. Department of the Interior, Bureau of Land Management.** The RGSS is **only used in 30 western and southern states**. RGSS divides land into **Townships** and further into **Sections.** These descriptions also use compass point directions *(northwest; southeast; etc.)*

> ➤ **Principal Meridian**: The vertical *(north-south)* line that runs through an initial point in the RGSS. There are **37 principal meridians in the United States**, each referred to by name or number.

> ➤ **Base Line**: The horizontal *(east-west)* line from which measurements originate. The principal meridian and base line cross like a "+" or bullseye.

> ➤ **Range Lines** are the vertical *(north-south)* lines that run parallel to the principal meridian every 6 miles.

> ➤ **Township Lines** are the horizontal *(east-west)* lines that run parallel to the base line every 6 miles. The township lines form strips of land known as **Tiers.**

> ➤ **Township** = 36 Sections consisting of a six-mile square or 36 square miles *(23,040 acres).*

> ➤ **Section** = 1 square mile *(640 acres).*

Example of Rectangular Government Survey System (RGSS) legal description. **Note: The written description is read right to left.** *NE ¼ NW ¼ Section 14, Range 3 West, Township 2 South.*

RGSS Sample Map Layout

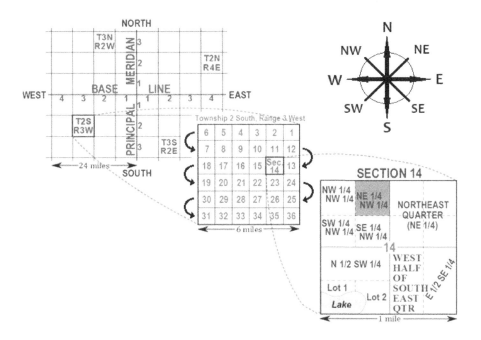

☑ **Test Tip**: Make sure you understand how the township numbers are laid out into 1-mile sections *(1 – 36)*. **Notice they do not read left to right but start at the northeastern corner and follow a zigzag pattern.**

Various Divisions of a Section

Sections can be divided in a variety of ways including quarters and smaller sections as shown below. The size / acres of a particular portion can be figured out by using the percentage of the whole section as shown below.

🔎 **Example** *1 Section = 640 Acres. ¼ of a Section = 160 Acres (640 x 0.25 = 160) and so on.*

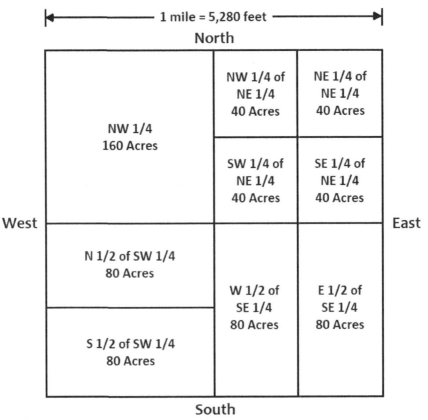

Lot-and-Block

Begin with a reference to either metes and bounds or RGSS, then divide the land into lots with numerical descriptions of each parcel. A plat with the lot descriptions is recorded in the land records. Lot-and-block divisions include streets, access roads, and other important features.

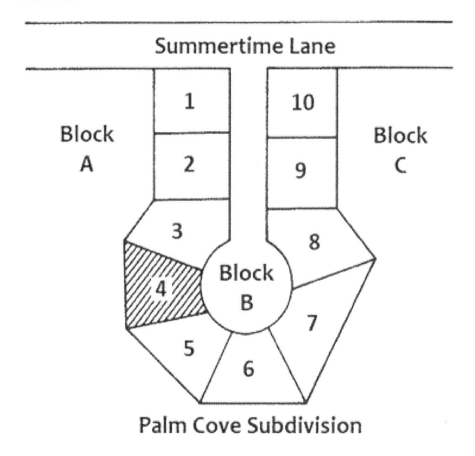

"Lot 4 of Block B of the Palm Cove Subdivision plat as recorded in Map Book 18, Page 11 at the Recorder of Deeds."

Points of Reference

Air lot diameters are measured based on the perimeter of the land parcel directly beneath. Air lot heights are established by the city or other governing authority that has jurisdiction. Datums and benchmarks are used to measure elevation.

- ✓ **Datum**: A horizontal point of reference from which surveyors measure the depth and height of various land elevations.

- ✓ **Benchmark**: A point where the exact elevation is known and marked with a brass or aluminum plate. Surveyors can use this as a starting point to measure other elevations.

Measuring Structures (Homes and Buildings)

The **American National Standards Institute (ANSI) Z765** sets standards for measuring structures. Structure area is stated in square units *(square feet, square yards)*. Structure measurement may be used to perform per-square-foot property calculations.

- ✓ Finished and unfinished spaces must be contiguous *(attached)* to one another to be included in the total measurement calculation.

- ✓ Finished spaces can only be included if attached to the main property via stairways or hallways.

- ✓ When measuring, round to the nearest inch or tenth of a foot ensuring to report square footage as a whole number.

- ✓ For detached structures, measurements are taken at floor level to the exterior finished surface of the outside walls.

- ✓ Stairwells and closets are included in square footage measurements.

- ✓ Treads and landings are counted in the upper floor's square footage.

- ✓ Ceiling height must be at least 7 feet to be included as finished square footage. Beamed ceilings must be at least 6 feet 4 inches under the beam, and slanted ceilings must have at least a 7-foot ceiling over 50% of the finished floor area to be included.

☑ **Tip**: When measuring irregular shapes, it's helpful to beak them into basic shapes *(square, rectangle, triangle)* to calculate the area of each and then add them together for total area.

Conversions

- ➢ **1 linear foot** = 12 inches

- ➢ **1 square foot** = 144 inches

- ➢ **1 linear yard** = 3 feet

- ➢ **1 square yard** = 9 square feet

Formulas

- • **Area of a Square** = Length × Width

- • **Area of a Rectangle** = Length × Width

- • **Area of a Triangle** = Base × Height ÷ 2

- • **Area of a Circle** = π (3.14) x r^2 (radius squared)

Livable Area *(Gross Living Area (GLA)* can be thought of as ***conditioned areas that are heated or cooled.*** This does not include *unfinished basements, attics, and garages.* GLA may include finished attic or basement square footage if ceiling height is at least seven feet. Covered, enclosed exterior areas are included only if they're conditioned using the same HVAC system as the other areas of the property. Additional finished buildings are usually included only if they're attached to the main house by a hallway or stairway. Questions on your national exam will tell you what to include in your calculation.

Usable Area is the tenant's specific space they occupy. **Rentable Area** is the total square footage that tenants pay rent on and equals the usable square footage plus the tenant's pro-rata share of any common areas *(corridors, meeting rooms, lobbies, restrooms, etc.)*

Appraisals

An **appraisal** is a formal *opinion of value* that a licensed appraiser assigns to a property. Appraisals are based on supportable evidence, as of a specific date, and in accordance with the **Uniform Standards of Professional Appraisal Practice (USPAP)**.

👍 Remember

- ✓ A real estate *Appraisal* is an estimate of current property value used by *lenders.*

- ✓ A real estate *Assessment* is an estimate of value to calculate *property taxes.*

Appraisers estimate the value of a building or a piece of land. They may specialize in either commercial or residential property. Appraisers typically appraise a property before it's sold, mortgaged, or taxed.

Valuation *(formal appraisal)* is used by mortgage lenders to ensure that the value of a mortgaged property is sufficient to support the loan amount. Lenders or appraisal management companies generally select and hire appraisers, but the buyer of the property generally pays.

Appraisers follow the **Uniform Standards of Professional Appraisal Practice (USPAP)**:

✓ **State the problem.** Identify the specific property, the rights associated with it, the purpose of the appraisal, and what type of value needs to be estimated.

✓ **Identify data needed.** Gather and analyze data. General city, neighborhood, demographic, and other data, as well as property-specific data.

✓ **Determine highest and best use.** What would the best use of the property be if there were no existing building on it? This matters more for commercial properties, though residential properties in a mixed-use neighborhood can be impacted.

✓ **Estimate the land value** *(as if the land were vacant).* Depending on property type use one or more of the three approaches to valuation *(sales comparison, cost, or income approach).*

✓ **Reconcile values to determine the final appraised value.** This isn't an average of the various estimates calculated. Reconciliation *(correlation)* depends on how well comparable properties match the subject property or could be based on the appraisal method used *(sales comparison, income, or cost approach).*

✓ **Develop and deliver the appraisal report.**

🔍 Example

An appraiser may use three comparable properties. One comp suggests a value of $735,000, another $689,000, and the third indicates $750,000. The appraiser will weigh the one which is most like the subject property more heavily than the other comparables in estimating value.

Estimating Value

- **Market value** is the most probable price a property will sell for in an open market if neither the buyer nor the seller is under duress.

- **Value** is a property's objective worth and may not equal price or cost.

- **Cost** is the replacement amount to recreate the property at current construction prices.

- **Market price** is the amount a buyer paid for a property and the seller accepted.

Factors that Influence Value

Location, Location, Location... For better or worse real estate cannot be moved and the amount of land available is limited. This is the reason why location is usually the biggest factor in value. Areas can change over time affecting the value of a property causing it to go up or down. Most people want to live in safe neighborhoods with good schools and easy access to resources. These could include restaurants, shopping, and local amenities *(parks, beaches, etc.)*

There are four characteristics of value that can be remembered by the acronym (DUST):

- **Demand**: How popular or desirable an area or property is.

- **Utility**: The property's function.

- **Scarcity**: Market supply, how many homes are available for sale in an area.

- **Transferability**: The ease with which another person can purchase the property.

Other Types of Value

- ✓ **Value in use**: What a property is worth to the person using it.

- ✓ **Assessed value**: What the local taxing authority thinks a property is worth.

- ✓ **Mortgage value**: Price at which the property can be loaned on or sold for at a foreclosure sale

- ✓ **Insured value**: Cost to replace or rebuild a property

- ✓ **Investment Value**: The return on investment a property may provide

A property with deed restrictions, outstanding mortgages, liens, judgments, claims, or other encumbrances against the property may suffer a loss of value due to the difficulty of being able to transfer title to another.

Economic Principles of Value in Real Estate

➢ **Anticipation:** Changes in value caused by the expectation of future events. Property value is created by the anticipation of future benefits the property may provide. Values can increase or decrease depending on the type of changes that occur. Physical, governmental, economic, and social changes all affect property value.

🔎 Example
Undeveloped land nearby an established area may see future development of both residential and commercial properties driving up the value of that area.

➢ **Balance:** The value of a property depends on the relationship between cost, added cost, and the value it returns. The 4 factors of production are: *Land, Labor, Capitol, and Entrepreneurship.* This includes the balance between the land value and the value of the home built on it. In general, the balance should be similar to the surrounding properties.

🔎 Example
A $200,000 home built on land that cost $600,000 would be out of balance and not bring the most available value to the property.

➢ **Conformity:** A property's value is determined in part by how well it conforms to its surrounding area. *Is the property in harmony and similar to others in the area?*

🔎 Example
A commercial property located in a residential area of single-family homes would not conform to the area. Incompatible land use negatively impacts property values.

➢ **Contribution**: The value of any given change to a property is dependent on the value it adds to the property as a whole. The cost of improvements does not necessarily mean equal value is added to the property *(improvements may cost more or less than the amount of overall property value added).*

🔍 Example

Adding a privacy fence and deck to the backyard of a home could cost $20,000 but increase the value of the property by $30,000. Finished basements, upgraded kitchens, decks, pools, fences, and garages are some examples that tend to add the most value.

➢ **Highest and Best Use:** Refers to a property's legal and feasible use that would bring the highest value to the property. The use must meet the following four criteria:

✓ **Physically possible**: An airport couldn't be built on an acre of land.

✓ **Legally permitted**: Must comply with any zoning and/or deed restrictions.

✓ **Economically feasible**: Market conditions determine the value of available options.

✓ **Maximally productive**: The best option that will bring the most value.

- **Plottage**: An increase in value that occurs by combining adjacent parcels of land into a single parcel. **Assemblage** is the process of combing the parcels. The value of the combined parcels can be greater than the cost of each individual parcel.

  ### 🔎 Example
  Combining three separate parcels that cost $100,000 each could enable more options for *highest and best use* increasing the total value to $500,000. A $200,000 increase in value above the cost of $300,000.

- **Progression**: The increase in property value from increased surrounding property values. Sought after locations drive progression. Value can change over time as market trends change.

- **Regression**: A decline in value due to the decline in value of neighboring properties.

  ### 🔎 Examples
  Externalities can cause progression and regression cycles. Since real estate is in a fixed location the value is affected by everything that happens around it. Zoning, school districts, nearby commercial land development, natural disasters, and interest rates all have an influence on value.

- **Substitution**: The process of identifying alternatives that would satisfy the same need, want, or desire. This gives balance to the available properties on the market.

  ### 🔎 Example
  A prudent purchaser would pay no more for a home than it would cost them to build or buy a comparable property.

➢ **Supply and Demand**: The amount of properties that are available for people to buy compared to the amount of properties that people want to buy. Location, scarcity, and desire drive demand. Real estate valuation can be greatly affected *(higher or lower)* in a market that lacks reasonable balance between supply and demand.

🔍 Examples

✓ *Buyer's markets* trend towards *higher supply* of available properties and/or *less buyers* looking for properties which *decreases demand.*

✓ *Seller's markets* trend towards *lower supply* of available properties and/or *more buyers* looking for properties which *increases demand.*

Sales / Market Comparison Approach

The sales comparison appraisal approach is based on the principle of substitution and uses the prices of recently sold similar properties to estimate the subject property's market value. The similar properties are referred to as *"comps"* or *"comparables."* The property being appraised is called the *"subject property."* Appraisers will typically select a minimum of 3 – 5 comparable properties after reviewing all nearby recently sold homes. This is the most common approach used to estimate the value of single-family homes.

Appraisers tend to look for the most recent sales of the most similar houses possible. The fewer adjustments that need to be made, the less subjective the appraiser needs to be with respect to the estimated value *(not cost)* of those differences.

Adjustments: Appraisers adjust the comparable properties' sales prices to make the appraised value reflect the differences in *features, location, condition, and timing* of the sale. Appraisers use analytics to determine how much these differences are worth in a given market.

🔍 Example
The subject property has 4-bedrooms and 2-baths. The appraiser uses a 3-bedroom 2-bath property that recently sold for $450,000 as a comp. There are usually multiple variables used for adjustments *(square footage differences, etc.)* To keep it simple, say everything else was the same and an extra bedroom adds $25,000 of value. The subject properties estimated value would be $475,000.

Bracketing is a process in which an appraiser uses *inferior, similar, and superior* units of comparison such as age, features, and transaction price to determine a probable range of values for a property. By utilizing bracketing, the appraiser can show that properties from a range of sizes, conditions, and quality of construction all indicate a similar value when correct adjustments are applied. There are two categories of comparison: **Units** look at the numbers. **Elements** look at physical and locational characteristics. The **Elements of Comparison** are applied in the following order:

1) Financing terms and cash equivalency

2) Conditions of sale

3) Market conditions at the time of contract and closing

4) Location

5) Physical characteristics

Cash Equivalency: An appraisal technique by which the price of comparable properties selling at different financing terms are adjusted to find market value.

🔍 Example

A house that sold for $500,000 but for which the seller paid $15,000 toward customary buyers' closing costs has the equivalent value of $485,000.

Cost Approach

The cost approach is based on the concept that the entire property is worth the sum of the **value of the land** and the **value of the improvements on that land.** The cost approach uses the following formula to determine value:

> ➢ **Replacement or Reproduction Cost – Depreciation + Land Value = Estimated Value**

Appraisers typically use this approach when the property is unique and is not being used to generate rental income. Examples include **movie theaters, hospitals, churches, and schools.** The cost approach can also be used in **newly constructed or unique high-value homes** that do not have comparable properties to estimate value.

Determining Cost

Both direct cost and indirect cost are included in determining construction cost estimates. **Direct costs** are directly related to the actual construction of a building, including labor and building materials. **Indirect costs** are expenses not directly related to the physical construction of buildings, such as permit fees, architectural costs, and builder's profit. The cost approach uses the following two methods to determine building value.

- ✓ **Replacement cost** bases value on the cost to build a functionally equivalent property using today's materials and standards. *This is the most common method used.*

- ➢ **Reproduction cost** determines the cost to build an exact replica of the property using current cost of materials. *Used for historically or architecturally significant structures, such as an old church with historical design and materials.*

Square footage method: The square footage of a structure multiplied by the construction cost for that type of building.

🔍 Example

The average cost per square foot of similar structures could be $250. If the subject structure is 2,000 square feet. The estimated value would be 2,000 x 250 = $500,000

Unit-in-place method: Combines the cost of individual materials.

🔍 Example

If the replacement value requires calculating hardwood flooring. The cost per square foot of installed hardwood flooring is calculated. If there is 1,000 sq ft of hardwood floors at $20 per square foot = $20,000.

Quantity survey method: Breaks the unit in place method down further to each component. In the hardwood example it would break down the cost of hardwood, cost of labor, nails, etc.

Index method: Uses the original construction cost *(without land)* of the subject building. An index number at the time of construction is used to offset the cost at the current index number. These index numbers are published by national companies that do the research.

🔍 Example

A property cost $200,000 to build 10 years ago at an index of 125. The current index is 150. Find the difference by dividing current index 150 ÷ by original index 125 = 1.2. Then take original construction cost $200,000 x 1.2 = $240,000 would be the cost to build the same building today.

Estimating Depreciation

The cost of recreating the existing structure or improvement is adjusted based on depreciation since the structure being sold is not brand new. The value of land *(as though it were vacant with no improvements on it)* plus the depreciated cost of recreating the existing improvement equals the market value. There are three causes of depreciation that relate to estimating value:

➤ **Economic Obsolescence** is depreciation caused by factors surrounding the property.

   A nearby airport or overpass that causes noise. (external depreciation)

➤ **Functional Obsolescence** is a form of depreciation caused by defects in design.

   Outdated structures or when a property is overbuilt for an area.

➤ **Physical Deterioration** occurs with wear and tear, damage, and improper maintenance.

   A deck that has not been painted or stained that is rotting or has termites.

Curable Depreciation refers to an item of physical deterioration or functional obsolescence where the cost to fix the item is less than the anticipated increase in the property's value after the item is fixed. In other words, the increase in value exceeds the cost of repair.

🔍 Examples
Repairing the deck in the example above may cost $5,000. However, having a functional deck may increase the overall property value by $10,000. Painting is another example that often adds more value than it costs.

Incurable Depreciation includes items not practical to correct. The cost of repairing an item exceeds the return in overall value it would bring.

🔍 Examples

A property with an outdated floorplan may sell for an additional $20,000 if converted to a more convenient open layout. However, the cost to make this change could be estimated at $40,000 exceeding the market value increase it would bring. Significant foundation repairs needed on a home often fall into this category as well.

The Straight-Line Method

This method calculates depreciation over time assuming an equal rate of depreciation annually. The *reproduction / replacement* cost, *economic life* of the property, and *effective age* of the property are needed to estimate current depreciation. **Economic life** is the expected period of time during which a property remains useful to the average owner. **Effective age** reflects how much of the economic life has been used and the remaining economic life for the property.

🔍 Example

A property has an estimated reproduction cost of $300,000. The economic life of the property is estimated at 50 years. The effective age of the property is 12 years.

Reproduction cost ($300,000) ÷ Economic life (50 years) = Annual depreciation ($6,000)

Effective age (12 years) x Annual depreciation ($6,000) = Total depreciation ($72,000)

Income Analysis Approach

The income approach is a real estate appraisal method that uses the income a property generates to estimate the fair market value of the property. This approach is commonly used for properties used as an investment to generate rental income. Examples include both residential and commercial real estate such as **rental properties, apartment buildings, condos, shopping centers, and office buildings.** Investment value can tell an investor the expected rate of return for a property. There are three different methods for estimating value within the income approach: *Gross Rent Multiplier (GRM), Gross Income Multiplier (GIM), and Capitalization Rate (Cap Rate).*

☑ **Tip**: A quick Google search will show you that the real estate world uses GRM and GIM numbers interchangeably *often referring to Gross Rent Multiplier (GRM) in annual terms rather than monthly.*

🔍 Example

You will see all over the internet that **GRM ranges from 4 to 7 are considered good for investment purposes.** While this is a true statement, that range is based on annual calculations technically referring to a good GIM range. This translates to an equivalent **monthly GRM range of 48 to 84** (*monthly income x 12 months in a year = annual income*). Make sure to clarify which method is being used when determining value.

✍ Remember for exam purposes

✓ Gross Rent Multiplier **(GRM)** is based on **monthly income.**

✓ Gross Income Multiplier **(GIM)** is based on **annual income.**

Gross Rent Multiplier (GRM)

GRM is typically used to calculate the appraised value of residential rental properties of *(4) or fewer units*. Nearby comparable properties are used to determine the gross rent multiplier (GRM) for the subject property. Gross Rent Multiplier *(GRM)* is based on *monthly income.*

Example

A subject 4-unit property has a total of $11,000 in gross monthly rental income *($2,750 per unit)*. Three comparable 4-unit properties are chosen. One sold for $790,000 and generates $10,000 in monthly rent. Another sold for $960,000 with $12,000 in monthly rent, and the last comp sold for $1,215,000 and generates $15,000 in monthly rental income. The following formulas are used to determine the GRM and estimated value of the subject property.

➢ **Sales price ÷ Gross monthly rent = GRM**

(Comp 1) $790,000 ÷ $10,000 = 79 GRM

(Comp 2) $960,000 ÷ $12,000 = 80 GRM

(Comp 3) $1,215,000 ÷ $15,000 = 81 GRM

Average = 80 GRM

➢ **Gross Rent Multiplier (GRM) x Gross monthly rent = Estimated Value**

(Subject Property) 80 GRM x $11,000 rent = $880,000 estimated value

Gross Income Multiplier (GIM)

GIM is typically used to calculate the appraised value of residential or commercial properties consisting of *(5) or more units.* Gross Income Multiplier *(GIM)* is based on *annual income* and uses the following formulas to determine value:

🔎 Example

A 10-unit property generates a total gross annual income of $240,000 *($2,000 per month per unit).* The property most recently sold for $1,200,000. An appraiser is estimating value for a nearby similar property that generates $300,000 in annual income.

➢ **Sale price ÷ Gross annual income = Gross Income Multiplier (GIM)**

   $1,200,000 sales price ÷ $240,000 annual income = 5 GIM

➢ **Gross Income Multiplier (GIM) x Gross annual income = Estimated Value**

   5 GIM x $300,000 annual income = $1,500,000 estimated value (subject property)

Reconciliation – A Final Estimate of Value

During the appraisal process, generally more than one approach is used to estimate value. **Reconciliation** is the process an appraiser uses to evaluate each approach to reach a final value estimate. The appraiser relies most heavily on the approach that best fits the subject property.

1) **Sales / Market Comparison Approach**: Single-family homes.

2) **Cost Approach**: Unique properties *(movie theaters, hospitals, churches, and schools).*

3) **Income Analysis Approach**: Commercial investment properties, residential rental properties.

✍ *Remember The values are never averaged.*

Capitalization Rate (Cap Rate)

Cap Rate is the annual rate of return on a real estate investment property based on the income that the property is expected to generate. This method is used by appraisers to estimate value of income generating commercial properties such as **shopping centers, office buildings, and large apartment buildings.** Investors use cap rates to compare one investment to another. A cap rate range from **5% to 10%** is considered *"good"* by many analysts. However, cap rates can vary by location and building type. Generally, a high capitalization rate will indicate a higher level of risk, while a lower capitalization rate indicates lower returns but lower risk. Appraisers often determine cap rates by looking at comparable property sales and their net operating income (NOI). The following formula known as *IRV* is used to determine value.

Net operating income (I) ÷ Capitalization rate (R) = Estimated value (V)

☑ **Tip**: If two of the values are known the other can be calculated.

✓ I ÷ R = V

✓ I ÷ V = R

✓ R x V = I

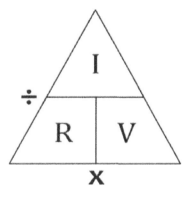

✏ **Remember** Cap rate, income, and expenses are *always based on annual numbers.*

Appraisers calculate annual income and subtract the annual expenses to estimate a properties net operating income (NOI). This is accomplished using the following steps:

1) **Estimate the potential gross income.** This figure is based on 100% occupancy. If every unit on the property were rented for a full year, how much income would it generate?

2) **Subtract vacancy and collection losses** from potential gross income. Refers to the normal loss of income caused by nonpayment of rent and periodic vacancies. This amount is usually calculated as a percentage based on similar buildings in the area.

3) **Add in other income.** Buildings sometimes generate additional income that is not related to the primary source *(such as renting parking spaces to the public)*. This is added to the remaining income resulting in the ***Effective Gross Income (EGI).***

4) **Estimate all building expenses.** Building expenses fall into (3) categories:

   ✓ **Fixed** expenses don't change with occupancy of the building such as *property taxes and insurance.*

   ✓ **Variable *(operating)*** expenses that are paid on a regular basis but may vary with occupancy. Examples include *utilities, management fees, landscaping, etc.*

   ✓ **Reserve** expenses are for items that need to be replaced or repaired periodically but not on a regular basis. *Replacing appliances* is a common example.

5) **Make the final calculation.**

   ➢ **Effective gross income – Estimated expenses = Net operating income (I)**

Comparative Market Analysis (CMA)

A comparative market analysis is a tool that real estate agents use to estimate the value of a subject property by evaluating similar properties that have recently sold in the same area. Real estate licensees perform CMAs to help clients make price decisions. They allow sellers to establish a fair asking price and help buyers decide how much they're willing to pay for a property.

🖊 Remember

✓ **Comparative Market Analysis (CMA)**: Informal valuation from a *real estate agent.*

✓ **Sales / Market Comparison Approach**: Appraisal of value from a *licensed appraiser.*

Selecting Comparable Properties

Comparable properties are referred to as **"comps"** or **"comparables."** They should be similar to the subject property in terms of *size, style, condition, number of rooms, and location.* Ideally **recent sales** *(properties that have sold in the last 3 – 6 months)* should be used as they reflect a more accurate market value than older sales. This is especially important in a changing market. A few months' time can make a big difference when the market is transitioning between buyers and sellers markets.

☑ **Tip**: Properties sold as *foreclosures, short sales, or other distressed property* shouldn't be used as comps unless you are pricing a property for sale under similar conditions.

Arm's length transactions in real estate describe the sale of a property where the buyers and sellers act in their own self-interest and are not subject to pressure from the other party *(usually having no relationship to one another.)* Sellers want to sell for as high a price as possible, and buyers want to negotiate the lowest price possible. These two opposing forces create a balance that determines market value. *Fair market value is the price a property would sell for on the open market.* By definition, fair market value is an agreed-upon price between a buyer and a seller who are acting independently without one party influencing the other. Other things then rely on that value, such as municipal transfer taxes and federal/state income taxes.

✓ **Arm's length transactions ensure fair market value.**

Non-arm's length transactions are purchase transactions in which there is a relationship or business affiliation between the seller and the buyer of the property. Below are some common examples of deals that are not arm's length transactions:

➢ Sales between family members or friends

➢ Sales between an employer and his or her employees

➢ Sales between a parent company and one of its subsidiaries

➢ Sales between a trust and its beneficiaries

Adjusting Comparable Properties

The goal is to determine a fair market value estimate for the subject property based on what a comparable property would have sold for with the same characteristics. Since the comparable property sales price is a known factor, adjustments are made for the differences in property attributes between the subject property and the selected comparable. Adjustments can be made for *location, property attributes, and market conditions.*

✍ Remember

✓ If a comp has *inferior attributes* to the subject property the *price is adjusted upward.*

✓ If a comp has *superior attributes* to the subject property the *price is adjusted downward.*

🔎 Inferior Example

The subject property has 4-beds, 3-baths, a 2-car garage, and is 2,200 square feet. The comparable property has 4-beds, 3-baths, a 1-car garage, is 2,000 square feet, and recently sold for $450,000. In the given area, an additional garage bay is worth approximately $10,000 and square footage adjustments are made at $50 per sq ft. The subject properties estimated fair market value would be $470,000 based on this comp.

➢ $450,000 (comp price) + $10,000 (garage) + ($50 x 200 extra sq ft) = $470,000 (value)

🔍 Superior Example

The subject property has 4-beds, 3-baths, a 2-car garage, and is 2,200 square feet. The comparable property has 4-beds, 3-baths, a 2-car garage, is 2,500 square feet, and has a swimming pool *(in a climate where a pool is a highly desirable attribute)*. The comp recently sold for $515,000. In the given area, pools are valued at approximately $25,000 and square footage adjustments are made at $50 per sq ft. The subject properties estimated fair market value would be $475,000 based on this comp.

> ➤ $515,000 (comp price) - $25,000 (pool) - ($50 x 300 less sq ft) = $475,000 (value)

☑ **Tip**: Determine the ***average selling price per square foot for the comparable properties.*** This is a good way to ensure the estimated value of the subject property aligns with the current market conditions. The median sales price per square foot of an area can be found by searching the real estate sites *(Zillow / Realtor / Redfin)*. Keep in mind these numbers are averages for a given area and there can often be differences in value from neighborhood to neighborhood. It's best to base value on the closest comps possible. Price per square foot is calculated as follows:

> ✓ **Sales price ÷ Total livable square footage = Price per square foot**

Livable square footage can be thought of as the ***conditioned areas that are heated or cooled.*** This does not include *unfinished basements, attics, and garages.* We can calculate the price per square foot using the examples above and include the median cost per square foot to compare.

> ➤ Inferior comparable property = *$225 per sq ft*
> ➤ Superior comparable property = *$206 per sq ft*
> ➤ Median area values = *$215 per sq ft*
> ➤ Subject property values = *$214 - $216 per sq ft*

Loan-to-Value (LTV)

The **loan-to-value (LTV)** ratio is the difference between the *loan amount* and the *property value.* Lenders use the *sales price or the appraised value, whichever is lower* as the property value. The LTV ratio determines how much of a down payment is required to secure the loan. LTV may also be a factor in the loan's interest rate, payment, PMI requirement, and loan type. *Lenders typically look for 80% LTV ratio or less.*

🔎 Example

A properties sales price is $575,000. The appraised value is also $575,000. How much will the bank lend if the LTV ratio is 80% for the mortgage?

➢ **$575,000 x 0.80 (80%) = $460,000 loan amount.** In this scenario the buyers would need to put 20% down or $115,000 to meet the LTV ratio requirement.

If the appraisal value came in at $550,000 in the example above, how much would the bank lend using the same 80% LTV ratio?

➢ **$550,000 x 0.80 (80%) = $440,000 loan amount.** In this scenario the buyers would need to put about 23.5% down or $135,000 to cover the difference in the sales price vs the appraisal amount in order to meet the LTV ratio requirement.

Private Mortgage Insurance (PMI)

Private Mortgage Insurance (PMI) protects the lender in case the borrower is unable to pay the mortgage *(borrower default)*. PMI is insurance coverage that is paid by the borrower to protect the lender. Typically, lenders require PMI on conventional loans when the **down payment is less than 20% and loan-to-value ratio is more than 80%.** This offsets the risk on high LTV ratio loans as they don't conform to Fannie Mae/Freddie Mac guidelines.

Equity is the deference between the **current market value** of a property and the **debt owed** on the property *(loan balance)*. Equity increases by paying down the principal balance and / or by increased property market value. Equity decreases by depreciation *(decrease in market value)* and / or taking out additional home equity loans. On a mortgaged property equity and loan-to-value (LTV) have an inverse relationship. As **equity increases ↑ loan-to-value decreases ↓**

Lenders must terminate PMI when the **principal balance reaches 78% of the original property value** or when the mortgage loan reaches its originally scheduled amortization midpoint.

Borrowers may **request PMI termination when the principal balance drops below 80%** of the property value. Depending on market conditions and property updates, this may permit borrowers to remove PMI earlier in the mortgage loan term.

🔎 Example

A conventional mortgage loan amount for a property is $315,000. The appraised value of the home is $350,000. PMI is required on this loan. **$315,000 ÷ $350,000 = 0.90 (90% LTV ratio)**
PMI ends when the principal balance reaches $273,000 *(78% LTV)* or if the borrower
request termination at $280,000 *(80% LTV)*.

Debt-to-Income (DTI) Ratio

Debt-to-income (DTI) ratio is the percentage of gross monthly income that goes to paying monthly debt payments. DTI ratios are used by lenders to determine borrowing risk. Buyers can improve their DTI ratio by paying off debts and / or increasing income.

✓ **Gross Income** is the amount of money earned before taxes, benefits, and any other deductions are withheld.

✓ **Net Income** is the *"take-home pay"* after deductions are made to gross income.

Monthly Debt refers to the amount of money spent each month on credit loans. Includes payments for *credit cards, auto loans, student loans, mortgages, personal loans, child support, and alimony.* Household utility bills, health insurance, and car insurance aren't considered debt. **Note**: Minimum required credit card payments are used, not the current balance remaining.

⌕ Example

$3,500 (monthly debt) ÷ $10,000 (gross monthly income) = 35% (Debt-to-income ratio)

Front-end DTI ratio only includes ***housing-related expenses.*** This is calculated using the future monthly mortgage payment, including property taxes, homeowners insurance, and any applicable homeowners association (HOA) dues.

Back-end DTI ratio includes *all minimum required monthly debts.* This includes housing related expenses and other debts like credit cards, student loans, auto loans, and personal loans. This is the ratio that most lenders focus on as it gives a more complete picture of monthly spending.

The maximum DTI ratio allowed varies from lender to lender. However, the lower the debt-to-income ratio, the better the chances of being approved for a mortgage loan application. Ideally, lenders prefer a *back-end debt-to-income ratio lower than 36%, with no more than 28% of that debt going towards a mortgage payment (front-end ratio).*

> ➤ **DTI ratio of 35% or less** is generally viewed as favorable, and debt is manageable. The borrower(s) likely have money remaining after paying monthly bills.

> ➤ **DTI ratio of 36% to 49%** is adequate but has room for improvement. Lenders might ask borrower(s) for other eligibility requirements.

> ➤ **DTI ratio of 50% or higher** is viewed as unfavorable. The borrower(s) likely have limited money to save, spend, or cover an unforeseen event. As a result, they will have limited borrowing options.

Principal, Interest, Taxes, and Insurance (PITI)

The most common mortgage payment includes **Principal, Interest, Taxes, and Insurance (PITI)**. Also known as a ***budget mortgage***, it represents the combined monthly cost of the principal payment, current accrued interest, and a 1/12 portion of the projected annual property taxes and homeowner's insurance bills.

PITI helps the buyer and the lender determine the affordability of an individual mortgage. Generally, mortgage lenders prefer the PITI to be ***equal to or less than 28% of a borrower's gross monthly income.*** PITI is used to calculate a buyer's front-end debt-to-income ratio. If the property also requires HOA fees, these are added to the housing-related expenses to determine the front-end ratio.

$\mathcal{P}$ Example

A borrower has a gross annual income of $96,000. Their monthly mortgage payment is $2,240 which includes principal, interest, taxes, and insurance (PITI).

> ➢ **$96,000 ÷ 12 months = $8,000 gross monthly income**

> ➢ **$2,240 ÷ $8,000 = 0.28 (28% front-end debt-to-income ratio)**

Escrow Accounts

Escrow refers to a legal arrangement in which a third party temporarily holds money or assets until a particular condition has been met. There are (2) types of escrow accounts used in real estate transactions.

✓ **Real estate escrow accounts** are used during the closing process on the sale of a property. The third party holds the funds *(earnest money)* until both buyer and seller have fulfilled their contractual requirements.

✓ **Mortgage escrow accounts** are used by lenders to pay annual property taxes and homeowners insurance bills when they are due. The escrow portion of the mortgage payment is calculated by 1/12 the total annual tax and insurance bills. This budgets a monthly amount to cover the annual payments that are due. Typically, lenders require a 2-month surplus to cover any additional expenses. Insurance and tax bills can change year to year, so the numbers are adjusted according to the latest bill. If there is money left over in escrow, lenders will issue the borrower an escrow refund for the difference. If there is a shortage in escrow, lenders will give the borrower the option to make a one-time payment or increase the monthly mortgage payment to make up the difference.

Earnest money is a *"good faith deposit"* a buyer makes on a property they want to purchase. Earnest money deposits can be anywhere from 1–10% of the sales price and are typically delivered when the sales contract or purchase agreement is signed. Once deposited, the funds are held in an escrow account. Ideally, earnest money is credited to the purchase price of the property at closing, but it may be used to compensate the seller if the buyer breaches the contract.

How Mortgage Interest is Paid

Principal is the remaining balance of a loan. In simple terms, it is the amount of money that's owed to the lender to pay off a debt. This does not include interest.

Interest is the cost of borrowing money that is paid regularly at a particular rate. In simple terms, it's a fee paid back to a lender for the money borrowed.

✓ **Fixed-Rate Mortgage**: Loans with a fixed interest rate for the entire life of the loan.

✓ **Adjustable-Rate Mortgage (ARM)**: Loans with interest rates that usually adjust annually, after an initial fixed-rate period of 3, 5, 7, or 10 years. The interest rate is typically lower during this initial period. Rate adjustments are made based on **index rates** from which lenders determine their margins and the rate charged per adjustment.

A **fixed/adjustable-rate note** is a legal agreement that permits the borrower to convert a fixed rate mortgage to an ARM or an ARM to a fixed rate mortgage under certain conditions.

Annual Percentage Rate (APR): The total yearly interest cost of borrowing money, expressed as a percentage of the principal loan amount. This includes any fees or additional costs associated with the loan. APR is calculated as follows: **APR = ((Interest + Fees ÷ Principal or Loan amount) ÷ Number of days in loan term)) x 365 x 100**

Borrowers can typically *lock-in current interest rates for up to 90 days.* As long as the property sale closes within this timeframe the interest rate will be locked in. If the closing date gets pushed beyond the rate lock period, then the interest rate may change.

Amortization

Amortization is a repayment feature of loans with **equal monthly payments** and a fixed end date. Monthly payments are applied to both the principal amount and the interest accrued.

Amortization schedules show each payment breakdown of interest and principal until the loan is paid in full. The interest paid is higher and principal payment is lower at the beginning of the loan.

The **interest and principal** have an inverse relationship. The interest applied each month is based on the current principal balance. Overtime, as the loan balance is paid down, the monthly **interest portion goes down ↓** and the monthly **principal amount paid goes up ↑**

A **partially amortized loan** includes partial amortization over the loan term and a balloon payment at the end of the term, where the borrower pays off the loan in one lump sum.

Negative amortization may be experienced with some adjustable-rate mortgages (ARMs). This occurs when a payment fails to cover the amount of interest due. When this happens the difference between interest owed and interest paid is added to the loan's principal.

Calculating Mortgage Payments (*Principal + Interest*)

Mortgage payments can be calculated using the amortization charts on the next few pages. The total monthly principal and interest payments are calculated using the loan amount and the corresponding annual-percentage rate (APR) / loan term numbers in the chart. As the loan is paid, the remaining loan amount *(principal balance)* is multiplied by the monthly interest rate to determine the interest paid.

🔎 Example

- ✓ A mortgage loan amount for a property is $500,000

- ✓ The **Annual Percentage Rate (APR)** is set at **3% for a 30-year fixed loan**

  (30 years x 12 months = 360 total monthly payments)

- ✓ The monthly payment can be calculated as follows using the amortization chart

  ($500,000 ÷ $1,000) x 4.21604 = $2,108.02 (monthly mortgage payment)

- ✓ The monthly interest rate can be calculated as follows
  3% APR ÷ 12 Months = 0.25% (monthly interest rate)

Amortization Schedule

Payment Number	Monthly Payment	Principal	Interest	Total Interest Paid	Remaining Balance
#1	$2,108.02	$858.02	$1,250	$1250	$499,141.98
#180	$2,108.02	$1341.53	$766.49	$184,696.47	$305,252.87
#360	$2,108.02	$2,102.76	$5.26	$258,887.26	$0

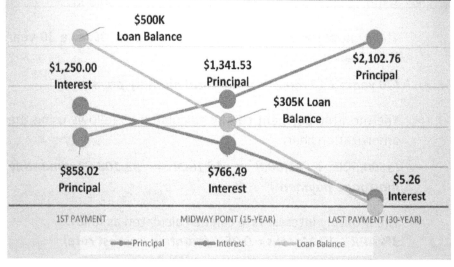

$500K
Loan Balance

$1,250.00
Interest

$1,341.53
Principal

$2,102.76
Principal

$305K Loan
Balance

$858.02
Principal

$766.49
Interest

$5.26
Interest

1ST PAYMENT   MIDWAY POINT (15-YEAR)   LAST PAYMENT (30-YEAR)

Principal   Interest   Loan Balance

Amortization Chart – Monthly Payment Per $1,000 Borrowed

APR (%)	Monthly Interest (%)	10-year	15-year	30-year
2.000	**0.16667**	**9.20135**	**6.43509**	**3.69619**
2.125	0.17708	9.25743	6.49281	3.75902
2.250	0.18750	9.31374	6.55085	3.82246
2.375	0.19792	9.37026	6.60921	3.88653
2.500	0.20833	9.42699	6.66789	3.95121
2.625	0.21875	9.48394	6.72689	4.01651
2.750	0.22917	9.54110	6.78622	4.08241
2.875	0.23958	9.59848	6.84586	4.14892
3.000	**0.25000**	**9.65607**	**6.90582**	**4.21604**
3.125	0.26042	9.71388	6.96609	4.28375
3.250	0.27083	9.77190	7.02669	4.35206
3.375	0.28125	9.83014	7.08760	4.42096
3.500	0.29167	9.88859	7.14883	4.49045
3.625	0.30208	9.94725	7.21037	4.56051
3.750	0.31250	10.00612	7.27222	4.63116
3.875	0.32292	10.06521	7.33440	4.70237
4.000	**0.33333**	**10.12451**	**7.39688**	**4.77415**

Amortization Chart – Monthly Payment Per $1,000 Borrowed

APR (%)	Monthly Interest (%)	10-year	15-year	30-year
4.125	0.34375	10.18403	7.45968	4.84650
4.250	0.35417	10.24375	7.52278	4.91940
4.375	0.36458	10.30369	7.58620	4.99285
4.500	0.37500	10.36384	7.64993	5.06685
4.625	0.38542	10.42420	7.71397	5.14140
4.750	0.39583	10.48477	7.77832	5.21647
4.875	0.40625	10.54556	7.84297	5.29208
5.000	**0.41667**	**10.60655**	**7.90794**	**5.36822**
5.125	0.42708	10.66776	7.97320	5.44487
5.250	0.43750	10.72917	8.03878	5.52204
5.375	0.44792	10.79079	8.10465	5.59971
5.500	0.45833	10.85263	8.17083	5.67789
5.625	0.46875	10.91467	8.23732	5.75656
5.750	0.47917	10.97692	8.30410	5.83573
5.875	0.48958	11 .03938	8.37118	5.91538
6.000	**0.50000**	**11.10205**	**8.43857**	**5.99551**
6.125	0.51042	11.16493	8.50625	6.07611
6.250	0.52083	11.22801	8.57423	6.15717
6.375	0.53125	11.29130	8.64250	6.23870
6.500	0.54167	11 .35480	8.71107	6.32068

APR (%)	Monthly Interest (%)	10-year	15-year	30-year
6.625	0.55208	11.41850	8.77994	6.40311
6.750	0.56250	11.48241	8.84909	6.48598
6.875	0.57292	11.54653	8.91854	6.56929
7.000	**0.58333**	**11.61085**	**8.98828**	**6.65302**
7.125	0.59375	11.67537	9.05831	6.73719
7.250	0.60417	11.74010	9.12863	6.82176
7.375	0.61458	11.80504	9.19923	6.90675
7.500	0.06250	11.87017	9.27101	6.99215
7.625	0.63542	11.93552	9.34130	7.07794
7.750	0.64583	12.00106	9.41276	7.16412
7.875	0.65625	12.06681	9.48450	7.25069
8.000	**0.66667**	**12.13276**	**9.55652**	**7.33765**

The 15 – 30-year columns show the amount of loan payment *including both principal and interest* per $1,000 borrowed. A new 15-year fixed loan with a balance of $250,000 at 4% interest would be calculated as follows:

(250,000 ÷ 1,000) x 7.39688 = $1,849.22 Monthly principal + Interest payment

Mortgage Points

1 point = 1 percent of mortgage
(or $1,000 for every $100,000 borrowed)

Origination points are used to pay the lender for the creation of the loan. These loan origination fees are ***typically between 1% and 3%*** and are included in the closing costs. These fees may be negotiable between the lender and borrower.

Discount points are mortgage points used to ***buydown*** the interest rate of the mortgage. As a rule of thumb, ***each discount point costs 1% of the loan amount and lowers the interest rate by 0.25%.*** Most lenders provide the opportunity to purchase anywhere from a fraction of a point up to three discount points.

🔍 Example

- ✓ A mortgage loan amount for a property is $500,000.
- ✓ The ***Annual Percentage Rate (APR)*** is set at ***3.5% for a 30-year fixed loan.***
- ✓ The lender charges one origination point to create the loan and the buyers decide to buydown the rate by paying another discount point.
- ➢ **$500,000 x 0.02 (2%) = $10,000 mortgage points**

It's important for the buyers *(borrowers)* to consider how long they plan to live in the home to decide if buying discount points is worth it. Based on the example above it would take just over 6 years for the buyers to reach the break-even point. Savings are accrued in the long term. However, ***opportunity cost*** should be considered as well. For example, the compound interest of investing that $5,000 instead of paying discount points could exceed the total savings. Especially, if the buyers do not plan to keep the home for the full 30-year term.

Rate / Point Cost	Monthly Payment	Total Savings
0 points = $0 (3.5% APR)	$2,245.23 (principal + interest)	N/A
1 point = $5,000 (3.25% APR)	$2,176.03 (principal + interest)	$24,912 (over 30-year loan term)

$5,000		$69.20		72 months / 6 years
(up-front cost)	÷	(monthly savings)	=	(time to break-even)

Calculating Closing Costs

Property transfer fees that aren't included in the sales price are called closing costs. Typical closing expenses include: *Loan fees, Title insurance, Appraisal and survey fees, Legal fees, Transfer taxes, Property tax and Insurance prepayments, and Real estate commissions.*

Loan Estimate (LE) estimates the closing costs within (3) business days of loan application.

Closing Disclosure (CD) shows actual closing costs at least (3) business days prior to closing.

A *Debit* is an amount that a party owes. A *Credit* is something that a party has already paid, an amount that will be reimbursed, or an amount that is promised. Common examples are below:

- ➢ **Buyer Debits** include *sale price of the property, appraisal and credit report fees, inspection costs, property and recording tax, title insurance, loan fees, attorney's fees.*

- ✓ **Buyer Credits** include *earnest money, mortgage amount, seller concessions (such as a seller paying some of the buyer's closing costs).*

- ➢ **Seller Debits** include *transfer taxes, real estate commissions , attorney's fees, recording documents to clear title, existing mortgage satisfaction.*

- ✓ **Seller Credits** include *sale price of the property, prepaid taxes or utilities.*

Allocating Expenses – Proration

Prorated items are shared expenses that either party owes at closing. They are prorated *(divided between)* the parties depending on when closing occurs. Prorated items will either be *accrued* or *prepaid*. Typical prorations include: **Property taxes, Rents, HOA dues, Water and sewer charges, and Utilities such as Fuel (propane or oil tank).** Mortgage interest and insurance are only prorated between buyer and seller if the buyer is assuming the seller's loan.

Accrued expenses are items that *haven't yet been paid.* In real estate transactions accrued items are paid by the buyer after closing. The seller owes their portion to the buyer at closing. These items are debited to the seller and credited to the buyer.

Prepaid expenses are items that *have already been paid.* In real estate transactions prepaid items are those paid by the seller before closing. The buyer will pay their portion to the seller at closing. These items are credited to the seller and debited to the buyer.

For leased properties, the amount of prorated rent owed by the tenant *(lessee)* is calculated based on the closing day *(start or end of lease agreement)*. If the lease is ending the tenant owes through closing day, if the lease is starting the landlord *(lessor)* owes through closing day.

> ➢ *Daily rent = Monthly rent ÷ Days in month*

> ➢ *Prorated rent = Daily rent × Number of days lessee occupied the unit*

Rules of Real Estate – Patterns & Percentages

There are several commonly used rules of thumb for real estate buying, selling, and investing. As you will notice they love to use percentages and numbers. Keep in mind these are general guidelines and often times there are many other variables to consider when making a decision. Also note that these will not be on the exam but were included as a quick reference once you are a real estate agent.

➢ **1% Rule**: Measures the price of the investment property against the gross income it will generate. For a potential investment to pass the 1% rule, its monthly rent must be equal to or no less than 1% of the purchase price. *($500,000 market value should generate at least $5,000 in monthly rent.)*

➢ **2% Rule**: States that if the monthly rent for a given property is at least 2% of the purchase price, it will likely produce a positive cash flow for the investor.

($10,000 monthly rent ÷ $500,000 purchase price = 0.02 or 2%)

➢ **4-3-2-1 Rule**: A theory that the most value should be attributed to the front of the site in the following proportions. The front quarter of the standard site receives 40% of the total value. The second quarter receives 30% of the total value. The third quarter receives 20% of the total value; and the rear quarter receives just 10% of the total value.

➤ **5% Rule**: Multiply the value of the home by 5%, then divide that number by 12 to get the breakeven point. If the monthly rent on a comparable home is below the breakeven point, it makes financial sense to rent. If the monthly rent is higher than the breakeven point, it makes financial sense to buy.

➤ **10% Rule**: A 1% increase in interest rates will equal 10% less a buyer is able to borrow but still keep the same monthly payment. It's said that when interest rates climb, every 1% increase in rate will decrease buying power by 10%. The higher the interest rate, the higher the monthly payment.

➤ **30% / 30% / 3% Rule**: Buyers should spend no more than 30% of their gross income on a monthly mortgage payment, have at least 30% of the home's value saved up in cash or semi-liquid assets *(20% for down payment / 10% in cash savings),* and buy a home valued at no more than three times their annual household gross income.

➤ **50% Rule**: States that half of the gross income generated by a rental property should be allocated to operating expenses when determining profitability. The rule is designed to help investors avoid the mistake of underestimating expenses and overestimating profits.

➤ **70% Rule**: This rule helps home flippers determine the maximum price they should pay for an investment property. Basically, they should spend no more than 70% of the home's after-repair value minus the costs of renovating the property.

Real Estate Math – The Best Tools & Resources

Real Estate Math Calculations

https://www.vaned.com/blog/real-estate-math

Mortgage Calculator

https://www.nerdwallet.com/article/mortgages/30-year-fixed-mortgage-calculator

Amortization Calculator

https://www.calculator.net/amortization-calculator.html

Proration - Calculate Duration Between Two Dates

https://www.timeanddate.com/date/duration.html

Simple and Compound Interest Explained

https://www.cuemath.com/commercial-math/simple-interest

Become the Go To Agent in Your Area

Think about your best and worst interactions with a business or service. What made them stand out both good and bad? It probably came down to whether or not they **met your expectations** and if you felt **seen, heard, and understood.** Make sure your clients feel this in their interactions with you. Exceeding expectations creates a lasting impression that continues to work for you long after the interaction is over. People get excited to tell others about great experiences with a service, product, or person.

"Seek First to Understand, Then to be Understood." – Stephen Covey

Clear | Competent | Communication – Be Prompt in your responses to clients, customers, and anyone you interact with during a real estate transaction. Go above and beyond to ensure everyone is on the same page and keep your clients updated on how things are going. Even just a quick message to let them know you are working on what they are looking for goes a long way. This doesn't mean you need to respond lighting fast to every call, text, or email notification, but make sure you get back to everyone. Ideally checking in before they reach out to you for updates. You could be hustling all day for a client but if you do not touch base, they can easily assume you are busy working on something else or have not followed up. You can be effective even with a lot of incoming requests if you batch and prioritize dedicated times to respond to emails, answer text, return phone calls, etc. Try using the ultradian cycles (45-90 minutes) we mentioned in the beginning of the book to block off time.

Become the Go To Agent in Your Area

Be Genuine | Be Kind | Be Honest – Play the Long Game – Each interaction you have with a client, customer, or prospect is a vote for the type of person you are. The more hearts and minds you win through your interactions the more they will compound overtime *(referrals and word of mouth)* fueling both your career and reputation as the Go to Agent. If someone asks you a question you don't know or need to clarify. It's much better to say something like *"That's a great question, let me find out and get back to you."* People genuinely appreciate honesty, and it builds trust in the person asking. Especially if you are speaking to them competently about the things you know. Most people don't do this because of ego and not wanting to look silly but it's a superpower in building trust.

Stay Curious | Be Open | Ask Questions – Build Knowledge – Research like a hawk. Everything from your local market trends, best real estate practices, anything that will improve yourself and your business. The more knowledge you acquire the more competence you build. Ask clarifying questions *(even to yourself)* about things you are unsure of, then seek out the best answers through conversations and research.

Due Diligence | Awareness | Composure – Master the Art of Negotiation – Find your clients Leverage and use to their advantage. Find out what the opposing side wants most and work to agree to fair terms. Be assertive but calm. Always maintain relationships even when a deal doesn't come to fruition. The link below goes into detail on tips for negotiating.

→ www.investopedia.com/articles/pf/07/negotiation_tips.asp

Helpful Real Estate Resources

National Real Estate Salesperson License Exam Prep

https://www.amazon.com/National-Real-Estate-Salesperson-License/dp/B0BSWQZTGL

PSI National Exam Content Outline

https://candidate.psiexams.com/catalog/displayagencylicenses.jsp?catalogID=337

Pearson Vue National Exam Content Outline

https://home.pearsonvue.com/getattachment/eec4b040-ad3d-429c-9eee-96c033d81349/Real%20Estate%20Content%20Outlines%20English.aspx

The Real Estate Marketplace Glossary: How to Talk the Talk

https://www.ftc.gov/sites/default/files/documents/one-stops/real-estate-competition/realestateglossary.pdf

Master the Art of Negotiation

https://www.investopedia.com/articles/pf/07/negotiation_tips.asp

Thank You!

Becoming a successful real estate agent is a journey just like any other endeavor in life. You will learn and adapt along the way. Easy Route's company logo embodies *"Creating your own Path"* which you have already started by taking the steps to become an agent.

Thank you for investing your study time with us. We trust that you found some valuable tips, tools, and insights. We would greatly appreciate your support by clicking the button below or scanning the QR code to leave a review.

Spread the Word ↓ We truly Appreciate your Support!

I wish you all the best in your future endeavors,

~ Easy Route Test Prep

Made in United States
Orlando, FL
21 July 2024